Citizen Science Skilling for Library Staff, Researchers, and the Public

Series: Citizen Science for Research Libraries — A Guide

Co-Editors-in-Chief: Thomas Kaarsted &
Simon Worthington

Series sections

Section 1: Citizen Science Skilling for Library Staff,
Researchers, and the Public

Section 2: Citizen Science Research Infrastructure

Section 3: Good (Open Science) Scholarly Practice
in Citizen Science

Section 4: Guidelines for Citizen Science Programme
Development in Libraries

Citizen Science Skilling for Library Staff, Researchers, and the Public

Section Editor Jitka Stilund Hansen

LIBER Citizen Science Working Group

Citizen Science Skilling for Library Staff, Researchers, and the Public

Section Editor **Jitka Stilund Hansen**

v1.0

Series: **Citizen Science for Research Libraries — A Guide**

Co-Editors-in-Chief
Thomas Kaarsted & Simon Worthington

Editorial Committee
Paul Ayris (Chair)
Bastian Greshake Tzovaras
Jitka Stilund Hansen
Kirsty Wallis

Reviewers
Sara Decoster & Stefan Wiederkehr

DOI: **10.25815/hf0m-2a57**

ISBN Print: **978-87-94233-59-0**
ISBN eBook: **978-87-94233-60-6**

Web: **libereurope.eu/cs4rl**

Source: **github.com/cs4rl/guide**

Published by
LIBER Citizen Science Working Group

Collaborations: **SciStarter; ECSA; COPIM (Community-led Open Publication Infrastructures for Monographs), and; Generation Research**

Template design: **Geralda van der Es/ SPRESSO**

Multi-format production
Open Science Lab, TIB – ADA Publishing Pipeline https://github.com/TIBHannover/ ADA. CSS template production **Interpunct Studios – Interpunct.dev**

Correspondence: **Simon Worthington, Co-Editor-in-Chief, simon.worthington@tib.eu**

CONTENTS

FOREWORD

Thomas Kaarsted and Simon Worthington
Co-Editors-in-Chief

The guide series *Citizen Science for Research Libraries* is brought to you by the LIBER Citizen Science Working Group. The aim of the publications is to provide access to the new open infrastructures and open science know-how that libraries have on offer for citizen science projects.

The guide is designed to be a practical toolbox to help run a citizen science project. It has been put together from contributions by members of the research library community and has been thoroughly peer-reviewed. The guide is part of a themed series of four sections based on the *LIBER Open Science Roadmap* that cover the essentials to support citizen science projects: skills, infrastructures, good practice, and programme development.

Researchers have been branching out into new areas of citizen science as digital services have pervaded many parts of people's lives, such as — wearable health tracking; data on COVID-19, energy, or transport; and for climate change mitigation and monitoring. Research libraries are in a unique position to offer up the frameworks and infrastructures built by the open science movement for wider use by researcher in society. In the guide series we are aiming to share examples of such projects.

Citizen science is a key pillar of open science. *The UNESCO Recommendation on Open Science* for the first time creates consensus on definitions and principles for open science. Citizen science plays a variety of roles in the overall open science endeavour of the *democratization of knowledge* such as — fostering trust in science, in data gathering and cooperations, and being more equitable — with our guide offering a contribution in capacity building for such values.

LIBER Open Science Roadmap,
https://doi.org/10.5281/zenodo.1303002

UNESCO Recommendation on Open Science – URL: **https://unesdoc.unesco.org/ark:/48223/ pf0000378381**

Image: Open Doodles by Pablo Stanley. https://blush.design/ illustration/i/NeXDqiwq2zFLGVeKIy3z All illustrations published on Blush can be used for free, Blush license https://blush.design/license

CITIZEN SCIENCE SKILLING FOR LIBRARY STAFF, RESEARCHERS, AND THE PUBLIC

Section Editor Jitka Stilund Hansen

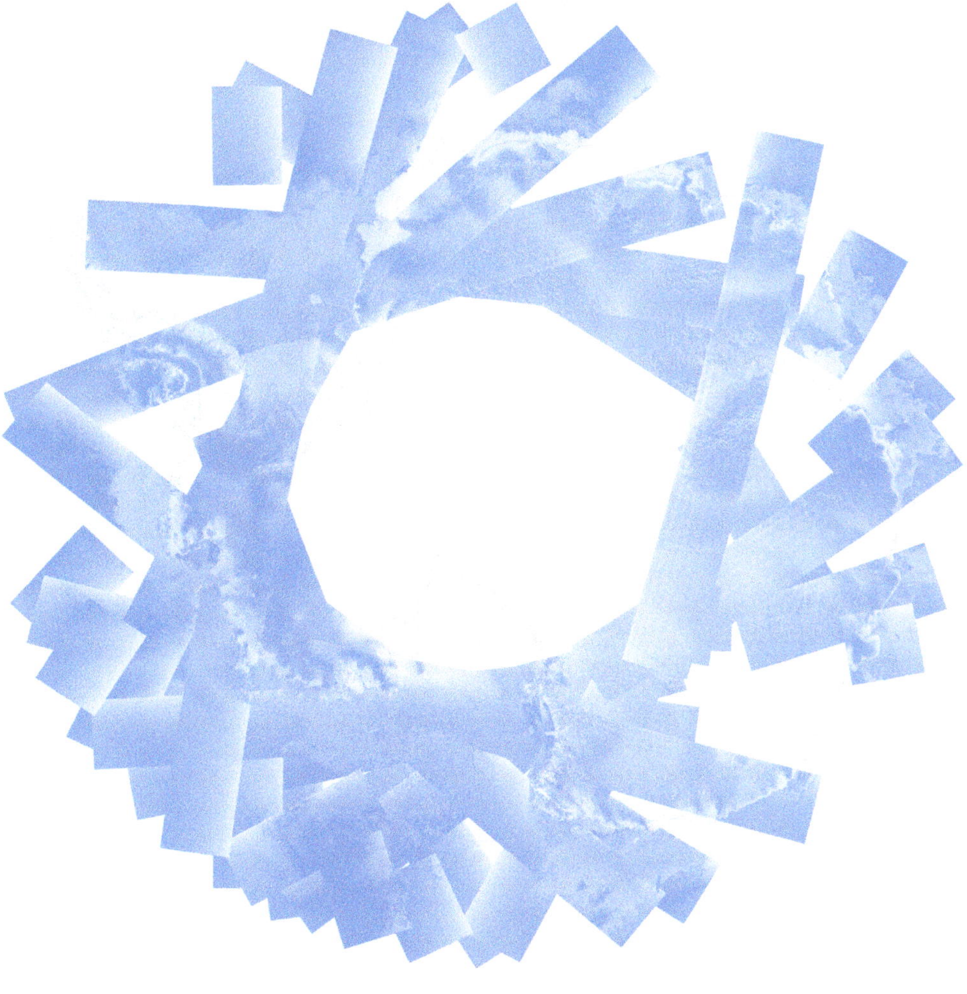

SECTION 1: INTRODUCTION

Citizen science as a scientific discipline is inevitably linked to the creation of data: identifying which data may answer your questions by using citizen science, attracting citizens and other stakeholders interested in the data, collecting data, telling the story of the data, and repurposing data. Citizen science can increase scientific literacy by use of data.

By Jitka Stilund Hansen, Technical University of Denmark,
ORCID iD: 0000-0002-5888-1221 e-mail: jstha@dtu.dk
Article DOI: 10.25815/rr9w-cw53

In this section, you will learn which skills can support a citizen science project across its life cycle and facilitate its success. These skills relate to project management, communication, management of research data and integrating scientific literacy into the project. Identifying persons and resources to the different tasks of the project already from the beginning may be a daunting task. However, realising and incorporating skills is a huge step towards creating a project that brings quality to not only the data, but also an experience of quality participation to the citizen scientist.

It is important to note that citizen science belongs to the open science domain, and is therefore perceived as a method, where research data are shared at large with open access to publications and full transparency of data availability. However, data use has to comply with ethical and legal obligations, such as GDPR, and with the expectations of the citizens. Accordingly, the FAIR principles do also have a role to play for citizen science data. The principles can help navigate the open science expectations and engagement of the citizens with the actual possibilities for sharing and reuse.

How to obtain good quality citizen science data is not addressed in this section, but it is inevitably linked to the possibility of reusing the data. A task of the research librarian is also to

This section will help you:

- Learn how **citizens and other stakeholders** have a role to play at many points during the project life cycle:

  - how they are involved in project management and co-creation,

  - how communication with them could be handled, and

  - what are the obligations pertaining to the data and knowledge provided.

- Get practical advice on **project management** and **communication planning**.

- Identify elements of **FAIR data** that require particular attention in citizen science projects.

- Understand how **scientific literacy** can be used for co-creation and education in citizen science.

convey to the researcher or project holder, why project management and good research data management practices are important: Quality data emerges from good management. If the citizen experiences that the project produces quality data fit for reuse and creating impact, this could empower the citizen and is a strong motivation factor.

> If the citizen experiences that the project produces quality data…, this empowers the citizen and is a strong motivation factor.

The skills highlighted in the section may due to their diversity not all be embedded in the research library initially. Therefore, the intention is to help clarify which support is already present and which skills should be developed or sought elsewhere. Hopefully, this guide can create momentum for the development of library services directed at citizen science. Academic researchers and project managers should be able to extract useful knowledge about management of citizen science projects and their data, and where to obtain more information.

Images: https://blush.design/collections/humaaans
Blush license https://blush.design/license

PROJECT PLANNING: A STEP-BY-STEP GUIDE

This project plan is a generic guide on how to run the practical side of a citizen science project with regards to planning and governance. It is based on the condition that a researcher or Principal Investigator (PI) leads the project. Assisting the PI is a Project Manager (PM), who is responsible for practicalities in close dialogue with the PI. The role of the PM is sometimes defined as Community Manager, based on the scope and communication of the project. Library staff in many ways are suited for the role as PM or project coordinator.

By Line Laursen, University of Southern Denmark, e-mail: linel@bib.sdu.dk and Thomas Kaarsted, University of Southern Denmark, ORCID iD: 0000-0001-6796-5753 e-mail: thk@bib.sdu.dk Article DOI: 10.25815/r3nj-fd31. The Project Planning guide stems from the work at SDU and the templates and tools we offer.

It's important that this generic plan is supplemented with e.g., a GANNT chart for organisational and time managing purposes, as well as other helpful tools such as a **stakeholder analysis**, **communication plan** and risk analysis. In some cases, the project plan cannot be outlined until funding is applied for and awarded. This guide does not cover that. Furthermore, if you are venturing in a multi-partner or EU project, this guide is hardly sufficient. It does also not take into account citizen-led or -initiated projects.

The project plan

Work on a citizen science project can roughly be divided into three phases. The BEFORE (**step 1-5**) where the project is initiated and planning is carried out. The DURING (**step 6-8**) where the project goes public. The AFTER (**step 9**) where evaluation, analysis, scientific outcome, and communication to and with participants is carried out.

BEFORE

Step 1: Definition of goal(s)

The overall outcome of the project is defined. This should provide a clear picture of what the researcher wants to investigate, who has an interest in participating and the goal(s) of the project. At this point, common ground is laid between the PI and PM in a dialogue with indispensable stakeholders, optimally including citizens. Which research objective or perhaps question is covered? The overall goals could be e.g.

- What is the research objective? How will it be investigated or expanded?
- The central elements with regards to public engagement and data collection: What is the motivation and outcome for citizens and potential partners. Already

at this point consider: What's in it for the citizens? This means that the scholar should explain how his/her research relates to citizens' preoccupations or areas of interest. An alternative approach would be to involve citizens in the definition of the research question.
- Internal goal setting: Aligning the goals and roles between PI, PM, administration, possible partners, and citizens.

Step 2: Stakeholder analysis
In order to operationalize the objective and goals, a stakeholder analysis could be carried out. We suggest **this template** in order to identify stakeholders and possible partners. Stakeholders can be very varied depending on the project and cover institutions, organizations, groups, or individuals that could have an interest or stake in the outcome or goals of the project. Stakeholders could also be researchers, peers, students or pupils (in which case the project could have a learning component).

After identifying stakeholders, a dialogue is established and stakeholders are onboarded. They should help form the project and outline their role. In this phase, 'must be' stakeholders who are critical for the outcome of the project are identified.

Citizens, of course, are at the core of every citizen science project. The steps above focus on organized groups or institutions that represent other citizens. This is not to marginalize the individual, but to suggest a structured approach. Individuals are also reached through the **communication plan**.

Step 3: Project goals and milestones
Once the outcome and stakeholders are onboard, the project timeline is defined. We recommend that the PI and PM spend a fair

Example of resources needed

In the SDU citizen science project **'Find a Lake'** (see also **communication plan**) citizens including public schools and high schools) contribute to assistant professor Sara Egemose's research into water quality by providing water samples and other data. From a resource standpoint the project relies on:

- The human resources include a main researcher (PI), a research assistant (community manager), students that do advocacy, a former teacher for didactic and communication purposes, an associated professor in charge of evaluation (science literacy), an IT-consultant in charge of the app, and a project manager, coordinator and web manager who also does visualization of data.
- The monetary costs focus mainly on citizen science kits for education and data collection purposes. The target group is kids and their families. Costs are also allocated for pop up events, camps and other equipment.

amount of time on a realistic and detailed plan that covers the main deliveries and assess the needed resources. A definition of the tasks and milestones (main deliveries) enables the PM to work based on a critical overview. A detailed timeline should include target dates and identifying risks. As mentioned above, a GANNT chart could be recommended. Also, data management is addressed. See **Management of Citizen Science Data** onwards. Quite often a research library offers specialists within the field.

Step 4: Assess resources and costs
Once the timeline is complete it's possible to create an overview of the resources and costs needed. Almost all projects come to fruition

after a potential lengthy application and budget process. Otherwise the budget is outlined by the PI and PM in unison. By resources we mean both human and monetary.

- Human: Researchers, research assistants, student help, communication, data management, visualization of data, it-infrastructure, and administration.
- Monetary: The cost of recruiting citizens, conducting workshops, town hall meetings, building apps, boosting via social media, producing video, buying equipment, tools, as well as travel costs etc.

With regards to human resources are the right competences present? Who does what? Occasionally, communication and community management are underestimated, leaving motivation and thus potentially data and outcome in jeopardy. This is one of the things to be addressed in the risk assessment analysis (step 5). At this point, it's important to address which target group or groups the project aims at as this is critical for assessing risk vs. outcome with regards to resources. Communication also comes as a premium. No later than this step, a **communication plan** is devised. A **data management plan** to overview resources needed for handling data and possible ethical and legal advice should optimally be drafted. You might also explore if the project could be evaluated by learning outcome or **science literacy** in case pupils or students participate.

Step 5: Risk analysis checklist

Risk analysis can help manage the potential problems and uncertainties in a citizen science project, including, where the a lack of skills or resources could become a problem. The analysis should be done in each phase of the project. There are a vast number of risk analysis matrices, templates and models readily available online. Very few, however, address research projects let alone citizen science projects.

Note: Some citizen science projects e.g. within health science have serious GDPR and ethic considerations. This should be addressed before the project is outlined as a very first step.

Below you'll find some observations and tips that can help structure your thinking. Risk, in this sense, is not meant as danger. It does not e.g. address unsupervised kids collecting data in a particular environment (although this is certainly a risk). The risk analyses should optimally be carried by the PI and PM together with staff with knowledge and insights in their specialist areas.

1. Brainstorm on potential troublesome areas. Every area should be included. From research outcome to data collection, to communication, retention and recruitment of citizens, to ethics, GDPR etc. Ask yourself: *What could go wrong in this particular area?*
2. What are the potential negative consequences? When the areas are identified, rate them on a scale from 1-5, where 5 is a risk that potentially can shut down the project.
3. How likely are the risks to happen? Again, rated from 1-5, where 5 is inevitable.
4. Multiply the numbers and you'll end up with a list of potential risks rated from 1-25. Again, a score of 25 might close the project.
5. Make a prioritized list. Which risks should be on the project's risk list?
6. How do you handle the risks? Some can be prevented. Then, they go off the list. Others can be remedied, and a Plan B can be ready at hand.
7. Make a 'go' or 'no go' decision, the PI and PM in unison.

This abovementioned list is meant for inspiration. If you work with e.g., IT-heavy projects or have data collection with potentially huge GDPR or legal ramifications, your university might be able to advise.

Images: All cartoons by Frits Ahlefeldt, CC BY-NC-ND 4.0, https://fritsahlefeldt.com/

Section 1 / Citizen Science Skilling for Library Staff, Researchers, and the Public
Citizen Science for Research Libraries

The risk assessment might cause a revision of the project plan (aim, goals, partners, roles and timeline). This is also discussed in step 6.

DURING

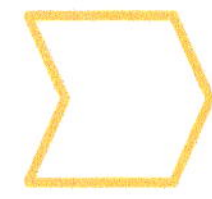

Step 6: Recruitment and retainment

For the research and public engagement side of the project to run as smoothly as possible, support from stakeholders and participants are critical. There are several ways to obtain that, but include both groups early in the conversation and co-creation by inviting to:

- Workshops and dialogue meetings
- Social media communities
- Info meetings
- Kickoff meetings
- Collect suggestions and discuss terminology and research objectives

Again, dialogue is critical which is also at the core of the **communication plan**. Get ideas, feedback, do post-its sessions, identify possible barriers and potential boosters. Be open and transparent on how you can communicate and include participants and stakeholders in activities, data collection and discussing the results. And where you cannot. The actors in a citizen science project very often have insights, experiences and connections into local communities, which are of high value.

Step 7: Follow up, momentum and communication

When the project partners agree on the project plan, it is distributed to all stakeholders and communicated to participants. In this phase, the communication plan kicks in. Including the ongoing collection, communication and sharing of data.

An example of recruitment and retainment

In the SDU citizen science project **'Our History'**, high school students interview elderly citizens on their life experiences with a focus on the changes in the family as an institution, work/life values and socio-economic themes. The project was originally conceived by Professor Klaus Petersen and three students from the SDU Talent Programme. Very early the project reached out to high schools in the region to establish partners. During various steps, a plan to embed the project in the curriculum was conceived. Similarly, the project (via the university library) built a digital learning platform that teachers and students envision will make them capable of conducting interviews in a semi-structured scientific way. Finally, besides the interviews themselves, the students will participate in a poster session where they reflect on the results. The point: It took several steps or loops to design the project with the aim of recruiting and retaining participants. In the end, all interviews are available online.

Image: SCANPIX

Depending on the type of project and the complexity concerning partners and stakeholders, status meetings can be held. They should as a minimum include the PI, PM, and key members of the project team. If a steering committee of stakeholders are formed, they are included as well.

Status meetings are for knowledge sharing, for boosting outreach and data collection, and potentially for discussing the milestones and revising the goals. These meetings should provide clear answers to whether the project is progressing as planned. An idea is to take stock of deliverables:

- What is planned for the next 2-4 weeks?
- Are there any critical deliverables?
- Identify possible delays or non-deliverables due to lack of resources.

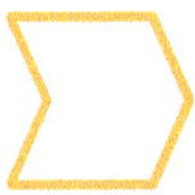

Step 8: Revision of the project plan

A logical consequence of the follow-up meetings may be revision of the project plan. Just as the partners and participants are visited and revisited, the idea is to establish a cycle where the plan is evaluated. Working with citizen science can be highly motivating and rewarding

for both the PI, PM and the project team (and citizens as well). Nevertheless, a potentially large number of partners and elements of co-creation might distort the focus, timeline and goals, thus causing unpredictability. This can potentially cause stress, missed deadlines and demotivation in the team as well as lack of communication with partners and citizens.

AFTER

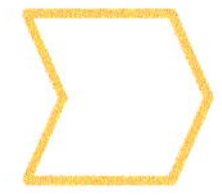

Step 9: Completion of the project

When the project period has ended or if the goals are met, the PI would want to end the project. In some projects, the co-analysis with participants are discussed or shared with decision makers within the field. In other projects, the PI and the research team analyse the data. In some cases, this might take months, but data and results should still be communicated with participants and data shared as openly as possible. Stakeholders and participants joined the project for a reason. Has the project created some kind of change? Could results influence a change in policy? Did it provide citizens and the research community with new insights?

Upon completion, there might also be a financial wrap and a report to various grant providers. An evaluation based on reach or learning outcomes e.g., science literacy would be completed. In conclusion, the collection of materials, kits and communication materials are done. Some citizen science projects are ongoing and the materials recycled, therefore, resources to secure documentation of the project and its data should be allocated.

Since projects might be repeated (or converged into new projects), it's recommended to do a memory log with members of the project teams. This can be quite simple, e.g. as a brainstorm. Name five successes or things to repeat. Name five failures or changes if the project were to be conducted again.

STAKEHOLDER MATRIX

When engaging in a citizen science project, collaboration and dialogue with citizens is at a premium. But which citizens to engage? Filling out a stakeholder matrix could be a useful structured approach to answer this question. The key is that citizens can be reached or included in groups or via institutions from civil society, private sector, government or the education system. Once stakeholders are identified, they might go into the **communication plan** as target groups.

Identify your own stakeholders from these examples

CIVIL SOCIETY	GOVERNMENT/POLICY
NGO's	International level
Libraries	National level
Associations	Regional level
Foundations	Municipalities
Cooperatives	Agencies
Trade unions	Authorities
Think tanks	Regulators
Clubs	
Churches	
Public service media	
Bloggers	
Online communities	

EDUCATION	PRIVATE SECTOR
Public schools	Businesses
High schools	Industry
Universities	Privately owned media
Night schools	Innovation hubs
Informal learning organizations	Crowdfunding hubs or platforms

COMMUNICATION

In citizen science, data is communication. Do not only regard data as the subject matter for analysis but expand it into communicable potential for dissemination. Citizens are curious and want to know how their data is used. Therefore, when designing a project, it is imperative you integrate communication as a tool for dialogue from beginning to end.

By Lotte Thing Rasmussen, University of Southern Denmark. ORCID iD: 0000-0002-5549-7208
e-mail: ltr@bib.sdu.dk
Article DOI: 10.25815/4834-zs30. This plan stems from the templates used at SDU for our projects.

Images: Undraw.co

In this section, we focus on communication with citizens. If you want to engage media or journalists this **guide** might be useful. Below we suggest two practical tools for operations:

- A communication plan
- A communication log

Communication to and with citizens

In citizen science projects, the citizens are more than respondents. They are participants who are invited into a dialogue regarding research. This dialogue can be conducted before, during and after your project [link: project management]. This is in order to create motivation, empowerment and potentially more or better data. Think reciprocity: the citizens donate data, time and energy. They should receive something in return. When designing your communication plan, focus on:

- **Engage in an ongoing dialogue *with* the citizens involved.** This can be via social media, your own channels, website, newsletters etc. and also by inviting media and journalists to join the dialogue. At the outset, communicate to citizens about the scope and goal of the project. During the project, inform and give feedback on the volume of data and be open about the analysis of this data, which they have helped provide. Create an authentic dialogue. If the data or analysis provide new or even curious insights (if not final), these stories might be shared and/or posted. Try to communicate in ongoing loops to demonstrate that their data and participation is useful.

- **Enable an ongoing dialogue *between* the citizens involved.** Very often citizen science projects create dialogue to collect data and enable co-creation. The knowledge and experiences of participants might be valuable. Therefore, it might make sense not only to think of communication as a transaction between the researcher and the citizen. Try to enable a dialogue between the participants. This might improve motivation, boost the collection of data and their possible interpretation. Think about communities. Virtual and non-virtual. Consider which communication platform would be most appropriate. Social media always plays a vital role today. Again, the more traditional media channels and journalists could have a stake.

Communication Plan (Citizens)

The plan can be implemented in the accompanying templates. Depending on the scope of the project other elements can be added. When identifying your target group(s), the **stakeholder matrix** might be a first stop. See the next Project Highlight for an example.

NB: The project might benefit from a communication plan for internal channels in order to target research communities, management, and groups of colleagues, etc.

Templates for the Communication plan

Target groups

	Name	Primary focus/message
Primary		
Secondary (if present)		
Tertiary (if present)		

Communications channels and theme

External channels	Target groups	Themes and messages
External channels meaning channels of communication that you can edit and post on yourself as well as channels where you might share content – or get editors or moderators to share it for you. Normally, projects benefit from establishing their own digital channels in order to reach relevant target groups. But channels can also be in-person encounters ranging from anything from workshops to town hall meetings. Consider creating information and contact materials. Both digitally across platforms like videos and photos but also in print like e.g. handouts, flyers or even booklets. Make sure to have clear visual design.	Citizens (participants) want an answer to the question: "What's in it for me?" Don't necessarily explain every aspect of the project. Begin with the target group and their primary interests. The operative word is dialogue. Meet the target group where they are.	Create targeted content. The purpose and the 'why' needs to be clear, when you are engaging citizens: "What is it we want?" A careful thematization with regards to the identified target groups including subgroups and messages can reveal opportunities for direct communication. Different spheres of interest would need different messages. All of the time consider what the citizen needs or is interested in — and what is irrelevant.
Web, including citizen science platforms. condary (if present)		
Social media		
Newsletters		
Other		

Communication log

In order to maintain overview and which methods and dialogue that work, we recommend doing a log of communication activities. What is communicated to whom and on which channels or platforms. The log will illustrate a progression or lack thereof and can be coupled to the collected data if the project wishes to include that. In the communication plan you write themes and certain angles that can be useful. In the communication log, you have the specific content.

Date	Channel/media	Content/message	In charge + status
Date/ week/ month		Primary content: What has been sent out or what is being planned, posted, published etc. Supplementing content: Photos, illustrations, datasets, models, diagrams, videos etc.	Responsible person Follow-up person Status on results

PROJECT HIGHLIGHT: FIND A LAKE

A Communication plan

"**Find a Lake**" is a citizen science project at SDU, Denmark, led by associate professor Sara Egemose. The project aims at involving kids in science in their free time. The goal of the project is for the researcher to recruit and educate citizens in collecting data of water quality and insect life to create a dialogue on future research questions. The project employs a range of citizen science components — kits, camps, pop up events, and has an app for data collection.

 Section 1 / Citizen Science Skilling for Library Staff, Researchers, and the Public
Citizen Science for Research Libraries

Description	Primary focus/message
Kids and their families	You can become a citizen scientist
Girls and boy scouts	You can become a citizen scientist
After school offers	You can become a citizen scientist
Nature guides and schools	This is an important and fun event
Public libraries	Let's do joint events and help us collect data
Think tank Denmark	Help us engage citizens and collect data
Local Newspaper	Help us engage citizens and collect data. Share data
Environmental agencies	We share data for decision making

Communication channels and themes for "Find a Lake"

External channels	Target groups	Themes and messages
Web	All	How to participate, information, booking, data collection, visualization of data
Social media	Kids and their families Girls and boy scouts Nature guides and schools Public libraries	You can become a citizen scientist This is important and fun Promotion of events, camps, Pop Up, Citizen Science Kits
App	All	Data collection How to participate
Youtube Channel (videos)	Kids and their families Girls and boy scouts Nature guides and schools Public libraries	What is citizen science? How to participate
Flyers, booklets and roll ups	After school offers	This is an important and fun How to participate
Citizen Science Kits	Kids and their families Girls and boy scouts Nature guides and schools After Schools offers	Data collection How to participate

MANAGEMENT OF CITIZEN SCIENCE DATA

In the following parts of the guide, we address subjects that will aid create FAIR data, but with an emphasis on challenges particular for citizen science.

Findability is addressed in **Section 2** of the guide about infrastructures. **Use of Data Policies in Citizen Science Projects** describes obligations related to Access and Reuse. You will learn about issues related to creating Interoperable data in **Citizen Science Data and Standards**. The **Acknowledgment of Citizen Scientists on Research Outputs** is very important for Reuse conditions. Lastly, you will find more resources and links in **Planning and Securing Resources — The Data Management Plan**.

(eLearning course)

RESEARCH DATA MANAGEMENT: QUICK START GUIDE

Introduction to research data management, the FAIR principles and writing a data management plan

Watch three short e-learning modules videos on Research Data Management, the FAIR principles, and Data Management Plans. You will get a general introduction to the concepts.

- **Module 1: Introduction**;
- **Module 2: FAIR principles**;
- **Module 3: Data Management Plans**.

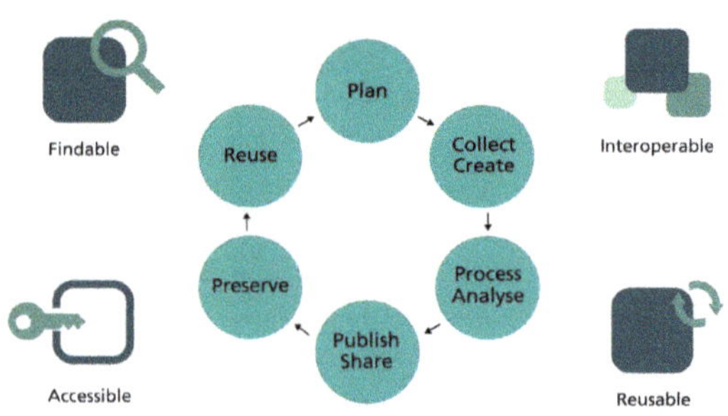

Holmstrand, K.F., S.P.A. den Boer, E. Vlachos, P.M. Martínez-Lavanchy, K.K. Hansen, A.V. Larsen, S. Zurcher, et al. "Research Data Management (ELearning Course)," 2019. https://doi.org/10.11581/DTU:00000047.

USE OF DATA POLICIES IN CITIZEN SCIENCE PROJECTS: A STEP-BY-STEP GUIDE

Librarians servicing an academic institution may be aware of legal and ethical conditions pertaining to research projects, but how will these conditions apply to citizen science? It is inevitable that project managers have to consider a myriad of issues about access to and protection of data produced or collected by citizen scientists. The checklist below may help sustain the engagement and trust of participants by adhering to ethical and legal obligations emerging in citizen science projects.

By Jitka Stilund Hansen, DTU Library, Technical University of Denmark, ORCID iD: 0000-0002-5888-1221 e-mail: jstha@dtu.dk

Article DOI: 10.25815/byq6-7095

Step 1

Manage personal information according to current legislation and responsible practices

If and how data can be accessed depends on private and sensitive information being embedded in the data. In citizen science projects, personal information (name, contact information etc.) of the volunteers and often location sharing must be protected and handled according to current laws. In the EU, the GDPR applies to all handling of personal data and includes data that can identify a person, but also sensitive data such as information on health, ethnicity or religion. Not all countries outside Europe have laws protecting privacy or sensitive information of participants in citizen science projects, so follow responsible practices.

Step 2

Clarify and review ethical issues

Evaluation by ethical committees are important for clarifying issues pertaining to health reporting and perhaps collection of biological material in projects, where citizens contribute with such data. Projects based outside an academic institution may experience difficulties receiving an ethical review depending on the regulation and possibilities in individual countries. Consider how participants are protected, their risk evaluated and how accidental finding disclosure will be handled.

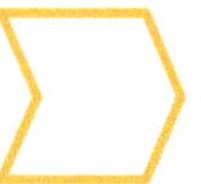

Step 3

Protect studied objects and populations

Sharing information about endangered species or particular populations requires special attention. Engaging specific populations in citizen science should be followed by clarifying their cultural needs during data collection and any resistance towards openly sharing (traditional) knowledge. It is the responsibility of the project manager to assess the consequences of data sharing and discuss this with the involved participants. Such issues may take time to investigate and should be planned for.

Step 4

Determine insurance coverage

National or institutional frameworks often insure and protect participants of conventional academic projects. This may not be the case for participants of citizen science. Determine if extended insurance coverage is necessary and how to inform citizens of risks related to their contribution.

Summary

The research librarian may readily assist in the practicalities of storing, sharing, publishing and licensing research data, and therefore also data of citizen science origin. However, bodies outside the research library often deliver legal advice and ethical evaluation of relevance for citizen science. Therefore, an important service from the library is to develop a framework to clarify ethical and legal conditions particular for projects relying on co-creation and involvement of citizen scientists.

Image: Undraw.co

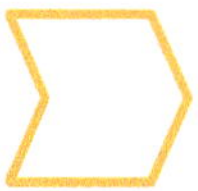

Step 5

Manage intellectual property rights of the citizen scientist

Citizen scientists may produce photographs, writings, and creative selections or arrangements of scientific data. In contrast to the undisputable regulations in many countries of employees' inventions, citizen scientists retain the intellectual property rights (IPR) to any copyrightable work they produce. Because the citizen scientists possess the right to exclude the project in using an invention they have produced, it is recommended to make transparent IPR agreements that are regularly updated with the participants. Also, the project holder should aim at sharing IPR, education or monetary value with the volunteers.

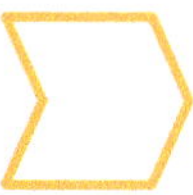

Step 6

Specify data access and license

Data without a license is not FAIR and the project manager should early in the project consider how access to data can be aligned with a usage license. Citizen science data may have broad applicability and such reuse is facilitated by choosing legally interoperable licenses for datasets.

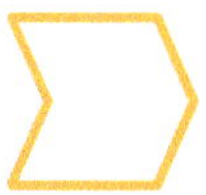

Step 7

Create a data policy and specify the terms of participation

Aggregate the above information and requirements in a Data policy and Terms of Participation. The information should be evaluated by relevant stakeholders of the projects (participants, organisations, institutions) before it is used. Participants must be informed about the Terms of Participation in clear and accessible language before they agree to engage in the citizen science activities.

Content of this section is modified from: Hansen, Jitka Stilund, Signe Gadegaard, Karsten Kryger Hansen, Asger Væring Larsen, Søren Møller, Gertrud Stougård Thomsen, and Katrine Flindt Holmstrand. "Research Data Management Challenges in Citizen Science Projects and Recommendations for Library Support Services. A Scoping Review and Case Study." Data Science Journal 20, no. 1 (August 18, 2021): 25. https://doi.org/10.5334/dsj-2021-025.

Also, refer to: Bowser, Anne, Andrea Wiggins, and Robert D. Stevenson. "Data Policies for Public Participation in Scientific Research: A Primer." Albuquerque, NM: DataONE, August 2013. https://old.dataone.org/sites/all/documents/DataPolicyGuide.pdf.

CITIZEN SCIENCE DATA AND STANDARDS

Three recommendations to cope with inherent diversity

By Sven Schade and Chrisa Tsinaraki,
European Commission – Joint Research Centre
Sven Schade, ORCID iD: 0000-0001-5677-5209
e-mail: s.schade@ec.europa.eu
Chrisa Tsinaraki, ORCID iD: 0000-0002-6012-0835
e-mail: chrysi.tsinaraki@ec.europa.eu
Article DOI: 10.25815/jqjc-qp38

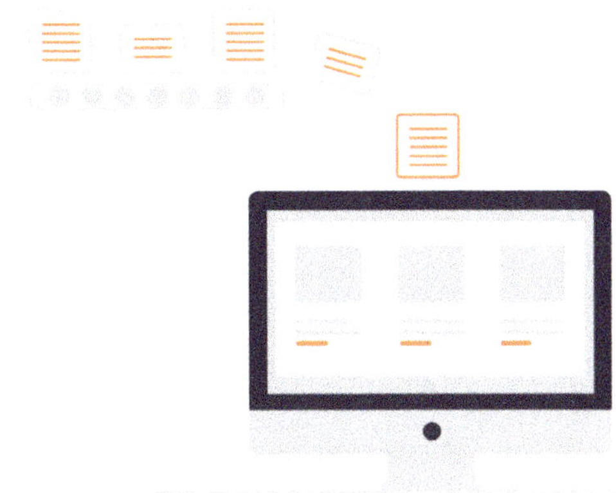

Image: Undraw.co

Applying standards to citizen science data is important for several reasons. First, the use of standard methods and tools to gather data helps to ensure the fit for purpose property, i.e., that the collected data meets the quality criteria of an intended use. Second, they can ensure that the data collected, validated or analysed in citizen science activities are provided under the appropriate access and use conditions — which hold to the participants but also to others (i.e., any third party that might be interested in re-using or replicating the work). Hence, standardization is essential for data to be reusable in other contexts. Third, the use of (domain-specific) data standards helps to ensure that the citizen science activity covers all important elements (attributes) of the phenomenon under investigation.

When it comes to specific (data) standards, there are many to choose from. In the context of citizen science projects, this can be considered an asset, because citizen science approaches are very rich and diverse, so that there cannot be a one-size-fits-all solution. However, a few things should be said about standards and citizen science data, and a few recommendations might help in advising practitioners and managers of citizen science standardisation initiatives.

Before anything else, the first recommendation is to avoid assumptions about any citizen science activity. It cannot be assumed that a citizen science activity aims at or would benefit from applying a particular standard, or that the participants are interested in data being re-used by others. Instead, the participants of any existing or new project need to be consulted to clarify their intentions and needs. Which (kind of) data will be collected or analysed by the project? For which purpose? What are requirements in terms of data accuracy, spatial temporal coverage? Who should have access to the data collected by the project? Are there any privacy concerns and which agreements need to be put in place to protect those contributing?

Regardless of the standard(s) that would be used in the project, it is essential to provide extensive instructions about their use, and to make sure standards are really understood and adopted by the different participants. Homogeneous data collection and representation are key for the overall scientific quality of the activity, so adequate training of participants will be utterly important. You can include information about standardisation in your communication strategy.

The second recommendation is to apply those few standards that indeed hold across any (citizen science) activity — and especially to the data it might create — those cover topics, such as:

- Assessment of the need for an ethical
  review of data gathering and treatment
  methodologies, including the protection of
  personal data. Existing forms (for example,
  **the dedicated online guide of the European
  Commission**) might provide valuable insights.
  If required, ethical reviews might take
  particular attention, for example to control
  if the people involved are informed in the
  clearest way possible (i.e., not only being
  directed to long and complicated legal texts).
- A careful assessment of the inclusiveness
  of the foreseen engagement methods
  and the way those are communicated.
  Here, it is important to clarify and clearly
  inform about conditions for participation
  but also which barriers this might
  create to particular communities.
- The explicit use of standards and, if applicable,
  of machine-readable data licenses (for
  example, **Creative Commons** might be used).
- Generic elements for describing data sets
  (metadata, such as Dublin Core) might
  be used in addition to any topic specific
  schemes. A first set of elements that
  are tailored to citizen science are under
  development **by the community**.
- For data exchange and access, it might be
  assessed if the use of de facto standards for
  the machine-based exchange of data over the
  web (e.g., JSON and APIs) would add value to
  the project. This should include an assessment
  of the available technical capabilities of
  the team. In any case, it is also important to
  ensure that data is provided in ways that are
  appropriate for the targeted participants.

Any additional advice on the use of dedicated
standards for data itself has to be put into
context. Standards for citizen science data are
highly topic specific, for example, different
approaches have to be taken when using air
quality sensors (see e.g., the **SamenMeten
infrastructure** — soon also in English), observing
birds (see e.g., the **European Bird Indexes**), or
collecting and reporting data about litter on
beaches (see e.g., **Marine Litter Watch**). The
odour pollution case description [link below]
provides some more details for one selected
example, but generally it is advisable (third
recommendation) to engage with research
institutions and/or public administrations that
are parts of the dedicated thematic communities,

Standards support interoperability among systems

The university library can be a hub of
knowledge for working with metadata
and data standards. It aids the academic
disciplines to identify and introduce existing
domain and community dependent metadata
standards. Find links and further resources
in the **DMP part**. **FAIRsharing.org** collects
policies, standards and ontologies from
different disciplines that may be useful also
for citizen science.

to learn about their standards and if and how
those might apply to a given citizen science
project. The best entity to engage with will
depend not only on the topic, but also on the
intended outcome/purpose of the citizen science
project. Public institutions, for example, should
be engaged if there is an ambition that the
created knowledge will affect policy-making –
and the right level of administration depends on
the intended outreach (local, regional, national,
European or global).

References

Schade, Sven, Chrisa Tsinaraki, and Elena Roglia. "Scientific
Data from and for the Citizen." First Monday, July 31, 2017.
https://doi.org/10.5210/fm.v22i8.7842.

Turbé, Anne, Jorge Barba, Maite Pelacho, Shailendra Mugdal,
Lucy D. Robinson, Fermin Serrano-Sanz, Francisco Sanz,
Chrysa Tsinaraki, Jose-Miguel Rubio, and Sven Schade.
"Understanding the Citizen Science Landscape for European
Environmental Policy: An Assessment and Recommendations."
Citizen Science: Theory and Practice 4, no. 1 (December 2,
2019): 34. https://doi.org/10.5334/cstp.239.

Hecker, Susanne, Mordechai Haklay, Anne Bowser, Zen
Makuch, Johannes Vogel, and Aletta Bonn. Citizen Science
Innovation in Open Science, Society and Policy. London: UCL
Press, 2018: 321-336. https://www.uclpress.co.uk/collections/
science/products/107613.

PROJECT HIGHLIGHT: DEFINING NEW DATA STANDARDS WITH CITIZEN SCIENCE

The D-NOSES project applies citizen science and co-creation approaches to set new standards for odour pollution — globally.

The EU-funded project **Distributed Network for Odour Sensing, Empowerment and Sustainability (D-NOSES)** is an excellent example of the diversity of citizen science and data standards. It addresses odour pollution with the strong aim to influence policies — within countries, the EU and across the globe. Accounting for around 30% of the environmental complaints globally, odour pollution is an unregulated issue in many countries. D-NOSES aims to create scientific references and replicability guidelines for defining new regulatory frameworks. Among others, the project **reviewed odour pollution and measurement techniques** and **compiled a list of good practices in handling odour pollution**. A related **Massive Open Online Course (MOOC)** was developed to support capacity building. The project highlights that citizen science can be an integral part in developing standards, especially in domains where those standards have yet to be defined.

However, a few particularities should be noted:

- In most thematic fields, measurement standards for data gathering and exchange already exist. Therefore, citizen science projects have different starting points;
- Regulatory impacts are not always the main driver for a citizen science project. Thus, different standards might be needed to address different ambitions; and
- Not all citizen science projects follow the same funding model. Available funds and related timelines do constrain the possibilities to learn to use existing or even to develop new standards.

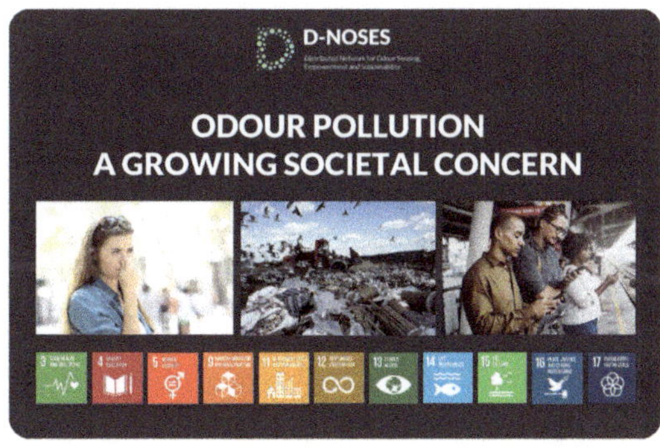

Images: User guide of the OdourCollect App; Policy Brief.
© 2018 D-NOSES. See: https://dnoses.eu/downloads/

ACKNOWLEDGMENT OF CITIZEN SCIENTISTS ON RESEARCH OUTPUTS

Providing credit where it's due, and how to achieve the 'Reuse' principle with information on data provenance.

*By Georgia Ward-Fear, Macquarie University, ORCID iD: 0000-0002-4808-1933,
e-mail: georgia.ward-fear@mq.edu.au*
Article DOI: 10.25815/rkzw-z561

Image: The Balanggarra Rangers from the East Kimberley region of Northern Australia. Image courtesy of Kimberley Land Council.

The 'Reuse' component of the FAIR principles dictates that data should maintain its initial complexity and have clear provenance information on how and with whom the data was formed. This, coupled with discipline-specific data and metadata standards, allows for data reuse in the future. Citizen science projects present unique challenges for accommodating the Reuse principle. This is because there is currently no single or standardised way for crediting citizen science collaborators on publications or datasets, citing collaborative works or providing Intellectual Property (IP) rights to the citizen scientists involved. Depending on the methodology used by the authors (or imposed by research journals), data provenance can thus be a subjective and sometimes mis-represented aspect of research involving citizen scientists.

Official acknowledgment for contribution to research is a cornerstone of academia and researchers should strive always to credit citizen scientists in appropriate ways. There are myriad benefits to official acknowledgment, some of which may only apply to the citizen science groups (e.g., unique funding opportunities; support to create formal structures around the citizen science group). In a collaborative project, citizen scientists/groups can be credited via the official acknowledgements, or via authorship on manuscripts/datasets. The latter often requires justification that citizen scientists have met the International Committee of Medical Journal Editors (ICMJE) standards which warrant academic authorship. Citizen science does not always lend itself to meeting these rigorous academic criteria. The case study below outlines a common situation in this respect and the diversity of considerations (cultural, legal, ethical) when deciding the best form of acknowledgement for citizen science collaborators.

PROJECT HIGHLIGHT: LIZARD CONSERVATION WITH THE BALANGGARRA RANGERS IN AUSTRALIA

Image: Herbert and Wesley Alberts with Georgia Ward-Fear. Photo by Georgia Ward-Fear.

To mitigate the impact of an invasive toad on a native apex predator in tropical Australia, a collaboration between conservation researchers and indigenous Traditional Owners (the Balanngarra Rangers, of the Balanggarra people) was formed. Each group brought their unique skills, experience, and knowledge to the project; an excellent example of the synergy between 'Western science' and Traditional Ecological Knowledge and skills. The research was highly successful and culminated in the development of a new national and international conservation strategy. The Balanggarra Rangers were pivotal to the success of this project in unique ways, yet crediting the Rangers was not simple. The group consisted of many individuals with varying degrees of input, and the group wanted to be identified collectively by their cultural name. However, adding the 'Balanggarra Rangers' to the author byline was rejected by some scientific publishing outlets due to editorial or ethical protocols, or because the Rangers'

lacked academic affiliation. Even those that did, reduced the author name to 'B. Rangers' in citations, an unintended but nevertheless culturally inappropriate practice. This experience motivated the researchers to petition for more inclusive academic authorship protocols that keep pace with the changing socio-political nature of research. 'Group co-authorship' is an option for including citizen science groups as authors, providing strong public acknowledgment and Intellectual Property rights. It also avoids some of the ethical pitfalls for adding individuals by name, who have not met ICMJE guidelines (which can be viewed as academic fraudulence). A summary of the suggested qualifiers for citizen science group authorship can be found in the infobox.

Research programs that engage with citizen scientists should identify the most appropriate method for credit at the outset. Not only is this ethical, but also helps to explore and achieve legal interoperability early on, i.e., the ability of organisations with different legal frameworks to work together. This may be especially pertinent in citizen science projects where disparate organisations, industry sectors or subsets of the community come together in a research setting. When assessing the best way to credit citizen scientists in a project, these are some of the questions to consider:

1. What are the wishes of the citizen scientists involved in the program?
2. Is the citizen science group readily identifiable by a collective name or could they create one?
3. Is the dataset in use 'static' (i.e., finished, whole and attributable to one group), is this a 'living' dataset and/or is only a portion of it being used?
4. Is it ethical or appropriate to identify individual citizen scientists by name?
5. Which form of citizen scientist identification will best support the 'Reuse' principle?

References

Ward-Fear, Georgia, Balanggarra Rangers, David Pearson, Melissa Bruton, and Rick Shine. "Sharper Eyes See Shyer Lizards: Collaboration with Indigenous Peoples Can Alter the Outcomes of Conservation Research." Conservation Letters 12, no. 4 (July 2019). https://doi.org/10.1111/conl.12643.

Ward-Fear, Georgia, Gregory B. Pauly, Jann E. Vendetti, and Richard Shine. "Authorship Protocols Must Change to Credit Citizen Scientists." Trends in Ecology & Evolution 35, no. 3 (March 2020): 187–90. https://doi.org/10.1016/j.tree.2019.10.007.

Hunter, Jane, and Chih-Hsiang Hsu. "Formal Acknowledgement of Citizen Scientists' Contributions via Dynamic Data Citations." In Digital Libraries: Providing Quality Information, edited by Robert B. Allen, Jane Hunter, and Marcia L. Zeng, 9469:64–75. Lecture Notes in Computer Science. Cham: Springer International Publishing, 2015. https://doi.org/10.1007/978-3-319-27974-9_7.

Group Co-authorship for Citizen Scientists: Recommendations for Using, Listing, and Citing

Group co-authorship should be used:
- When the group in question expresses a desire for authorship.
- When groups cannot meet ICMJE or journal specific standards but their contribution was deemed essential to the success of the project. For citizen science projects, this should include 'data acquisition', which would not normally warrant authorship alone.
- Only for established groups (e.g., the 'Balanggarra Rangers') not for amorphous groups who engage with generic surveys or medical studies. Such groups are best recognised in the Acknowledgment section.

Group co-author names should:
- Be as short as possible, and
- be listed in full at all times (e.g., 'Balanggarra Rangers' not 'B. Rangers') i.e., both in the author byline and also when citing and indexing in references. This is also the responsibility of the publisher and indexing programs/institutions.

All authors collectively decide:
- On the best form of acknowledgment and whether it meets the 'Reuse' principle.
- The most appropriate order of authorship (groups co-authors can be anywhere in that order).
- Whether to list individual citizen scientist names elsewhere in the text (e.g., supplementary materials or appendices), remembering that some citizen scientists may be eligible for individual authorship independent of the group. Group co-authorship doesn't replace this option.

Adapted from Ward-Fear et al. 2020

PLANNING AND SECURING RESOURCES — THE DATA MANAGEMENT PLAN

By Iryna Kuchma, Electronic Information for Libraries,
ORCID iD: 0000-0002-2064-3439
e-mail: iryna.kuchma@eifl.net
Article DOI: 10.20389/tpap-md16

Image: eLearning course about the importance of good research data management (RDM). https://doi.org/10.11581/DTU:00000047

A data management plan (DMP) can support citizen science data in becoming FAIR. It should be created early in the research process and updated regularly to prepare for data deposit, sharing and reuse. University libraries already have knowledge of FAIR data. So in this final part about the DMP, we emphasize resources useful for citizen science projects and in which sections of the guide, you can find related information. A common understanding of how data will be managed is particularly important in collaborative projects that involve researchers, institutions and groups with different ways of working and expectations.

This guidance follows the six Science Europe core requirements for DMPs (Science Europe 2021). Also, refer to Wiggins et al. (2013) for writing a DMP for citizen science projects.

Find **a curated collection of Horizon 2020 DMPs** where several address citizen science projects. If your research library does not provide a DMP tool, use free online tools for writing DMPs such as **ARGOS** or **DMPOnline**.

1. Data description and collection or re-use of existing data

The data description is the core part that you build upon to make decisions on data management. In this section you include information on the type of data that will be gathered. To increase the value of citizen science data from the perspective of the general public (community interoperability) or regulatory authorities, interoperable data should be planned for. This is important for integration with existing data or when using existing technologies for data collection.

Learn more about **Citizen Science Data and Standards** and about **open science**.

2. Documentation and data quality

Describing why and how data was collected is important for documenting the data quality. The data handling skills of the participants may be unknown, therefore, describe methods used to collect and treat data, data provenance, and quality-assurance steps taken. Explain how you will guarantee consistency within your dataset. Metadata standards from relevant disciplines (if existing) are key for data interoperability and reuse. Ventures in new technology should aim at following community standards and being open source so later users can implement and further develop the tools to their needs.

Learn more about **Citizen Science Data and Standards**. Search **FAIRsharing** for standards, ontologies and policies.

3. Storage and backup during the research process

It is good practice to store data in at least one non-proprietary format. Project managers often use their personal data storage and the library role could be to help with the institutional storage provisions or identifying infrastructures fit for citizen science data. Seek storage solutions, which offer flexibility and protection for sensitive data or data with disclosure risk. Best practice is to store data without direct identifiers and replace personal identifiers with a randomly assigned identifier (ask researchers to create a separate file, to be kept apart from the rest of the data, which provides the linking relationship between any personal identifiers and the randomly assigned unique identifiers). Where possible, select a storage solution that allows an easy way to maintain version control.

Learn more about infrastructures for Citizen Science in **Section 2** of this guide.

4. Legal and ethical requirements, codes of conduct

Citizen science projects might not have access to legal and ethical advice, and may need help to establish approval mechanisms for sharing data (via consent, regulation, institutional agreements and other systematic data governance mechanisms, including restricted access conditions and embargoes if required). Acknowledge data provenance in metadata and any limitations or obligations in secondary use, inclusive of issues of consent.

Learn more in **Use of Data Policies in Citizen Science Projects** and **Acknowledgment of Citizen Scientists on Research Outputs**.

5. Data sharing and long-term preservation

Where possible, advice to provide immediate open access to citizen science data and recommend Creative Commons Attribution 4.0 International License (CC BY 4.0), a Creative Commons Public Domain Dedication or equivalent. Also, clarify whether any project funder has specific data access requirements. Know the needs of the participants before you share any data and determine methods for sharing. If immediate open access is not possible, consider creating a metadata record in a repository where a persistent identifier and license can be assigned. If data cannot be open, indicate how they can be made accessible, and under which conditions. Describe which measures you will take to enable long-term preservation.

Remember to consult your participants during the **project planning** and with regard to their expectations of data sharing (see **Citizen Science Data and Standards**).
Get more information about **Use of Data Policies in Citizen Science Projects** and about infrastructures for sharing data in **Section 2**.

6. Data management responsibilities and resources

Describe who (for example role, position, and institution) will be responsible for data management. What resources (for example financial and time) will be dedicated to data management and ensuring that data will be FAIR. Apps or technologies for data collection and participant interaction may require regular maintenance and updates – and therefore, funding for long-term support. By planning early, costs can be significantly reduced.

Identify and assess **RDM costs** and include them in the **project planning**.

References

Science Europe. Practical Guide to the International Alignment of Research Data Management. (Extended Edition). Brussels: Science Europe, 2021. https://www.scienceeurope.org/media/4brkxxe5/se_rdm_practical_guide_extended_final.pdf.

Wiggins, A, Bonney, R, Graham, E, Henderson, S, Kelling, S, Littauer, R, Lebuhn, G, Lotts, G, Michener, W, Newman, G, Russel, E, Stevenson, R, Weltzin, J. Data Management Guide for Public Participation in Scientific Research. DataOne, 2013 http://safmc.net/wp-content/uploads/2016/06/Wigginsetal2013_DataManagementGuidePPSR.pd

PROJECT HIGHLIGHT: FAIR DATA IN A CITIZEN SCIENCE PROJECT

Article DOI: *10.25815/tnrh-zg50*

Fangstjournalen is a citizen science project highlighting several of the points from this section: it demonstrates how good communication, project and data management create value to citizen scientists and also to scientific data. Learn how the project manager makes his data FAIR and share data with the citizens in this short video (Holmstrand et al. 2020). The collected data are relevant for reuse in projects about biodiversity, behavior and recreation, but also for national fishery regulation and policy development. Due to the content of personal data, the database is not shared openly but via a metadata record (Skov 2021).

References

Holmstrand, Katrine Flindt, Asger Væring Larsen, Signe Gadegaard, Jitka Stilund Hansen, Karsten Kryger Hansen, and Gertrud Stougård Thomsen. "FAIR Data in a Citizen Science Project 'Fangstjournalen,'" 2020. https://doi.org/10.11581/DTU:00000092.

Skov, Christian. "Database from Citizen Science Project 'Fangstjournalen.'" Technical University of Denmark, 2021. https://doi.org/10.11583/DTU.13795928.

Image: Fangstjournalen – registration of catches by recreational anglers. Photo by Christian Skov, ORCID iD: 0000-0002-8547-6520 CCBY- SA 2.0.

PROJECT HIGHLIGHT: THE INOS PROJECT

Article DOI: 10.25815/aayw-w097

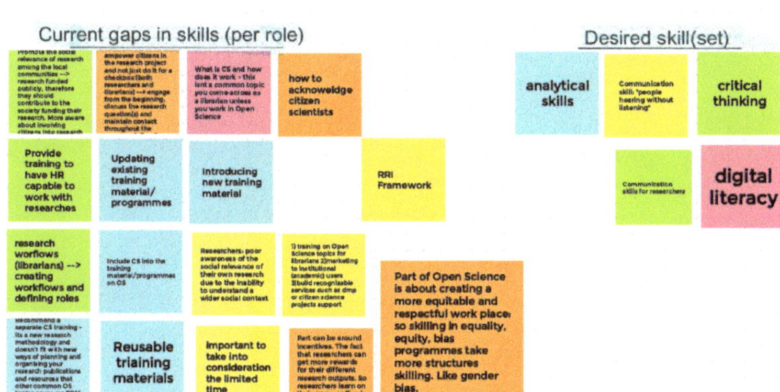

The INOS project is funded under the Erasmus+ KA2 Strategic Partnerships program and aims at integrating open science and citizen science into active learning approaches in Higher Education. INOS is a partnership of four universities (Aalborg University, Tallinn University, University of Oulu, University of Bordeaux), an SME (Web2Learn) and LIBER the Association of European Research Libraries.

Upskilling through open knowledge activities

In its three year duration and among its other goals and activities, INOS aims to expose academic and library staff and students to participatory methods in fostering open science, and consequently upskill them, so that they reflect on updating pedagogical models in Higher Education through citizen science. It does so by encouraging universities and university libraries to co-create and participate in Open Knowledge and Open Innovation activities. In this context LIBER co-organised four Open Knowledge Activities (OKAs) with five LIBER participant libraries and with the support of the LIBER Citizen Science Working Group and the LIBER Copyright and Legal Matters Working Group. The LIBER OKAs aimed at co-creating and debating on citizen science concepts, thus upskilling the participants in open and citizen science.

Towards a Roadmap on Capacity Building on Open Science and Citizen Science for Research Libraries — Co-creating a vision

Building up on the project's overall intellectual outputs and activities, LIBER is leading activities on engagement, awareness raising and fostering policy change. In this framework, LIBER has recently organised two highly interactive vision-building workshops that led to the publication of a report on co-creating a vision for citizen science in higher education. This activity, together with the previous OKAs, are the starting point for a workshop dedicated to research libraries, aiming to co-create a Roadmap on Capacity Building on Open Science and Citizen Science for Research Libraries. The project will wrap up its activities with a report the the final Stakeholders' Consultation of the project and its final Vision and Policy Recommendations for Higher Education.

Web: **https://inos-project.eu/**

INCREASING SCIENTIFIC LITERACY WITH CITIZEN SCIENCE

Citizen science has the potential to sustain the citizen in developing scientific skills and to increase public understanding of science. Thus, scientific literacy can be an integral part of citizen science projects.

By Berit Elisabeth Alving, University of Southern Denmark,
ORCID iD: 0000-0002-4708-5000 e-mail: balving@bib.sdu.dk
Article DOI: 10.20389/dnnk-tv30

Scientific literacy and citizen science

Citizens who are scientific literate can contribute and collect data in a useful and qualified way in e.g., citizen science projects and can to a greater extent use scientific methods and make informed decisions. Some citizen science projects can even increase the participants' scientific literacy, if projects may contain elements of empowerment, inclusion, and motivation. For citizens to acquire knowledge and thus, become more literate, the citizen science projects must be relevant and preferably related to the citizens' local environment. Personal involvement and interests makes people more motivated, and thus more likely to seek information. Effects of citizen science projects on scientific literacy could be better comprehension of scientific information and scientific processes and a change in attitudes towards science. The citizens may engage more in science or even consider science as a career.

Research libraries and scientific literacy

The libraries' mission to promote and provide tools and resources to master scientific information and information literacy, even scientific literacy, matches the citizen science projects, where citizens acquire scientific skills in observing, deriving, predicting, and making sense of collected data and observations. By connecting scientific researchers with scientific literate citizens, the library could become a channel for citizen science projects, as well as an intellectual hub. The library will be a place to access and use scientific information as well as to create and engage in scientific endeavours.

Definition of Scientific Literacy

Scientific literacy is knowledge and understanding of scientific concepts, processes, and methods, giving you the ability to discuss and evaluate the origin and quality of scientific results and thus seek answers to scientific questions. The scientific literate citizen can distinguish science from pseudoscience.

The University Library of Southern Denmark is a partner of citizen science projects and several of these involve pupils from elementary schools and high schools. In one project, "A Healthier Southern Denmark", high school classes were involved and learned about health science and the library held a course in critical source reading as a supplement to the students' curriculum. Another example from the university library is the project "Find a lake", where elementary school pupils test the quality of the water. The latter had a goal to educate the pupils to be responsible citizens through insight on humans' impact on nature. The pupils were highly motivated and the purpose of the projects was clear and relevant to them. Both projects and the educational material were a co-creation between the schools, the researchers, and the university library. The library acted as a link between the schools and the researchers.

References

Golumbic, Yaela N., Barak Fishbain, and Ayelet Baram-Tsabari. "Science Literacy in Action: Understanding Scientific Data Presented in a Citizen Science Platform by Non-Expert Adults." International Journal of Science Education, Part B 10, no. 3 (July 2, 2020): 232–47. https://doi.org/10.1080/21548455.2020.1769877.

Shaffer, Justin F., Julie Ferguson, and Kameryn Denaro. "Use of the Test of Scientific Literacy Skills Reveals That Fundamental Literacy Is an Important Contributor to Scientific Literacy." Edited by Peggy Brickman. CBE—Life Sciences Education 18, no. 3 (September 2019): ar31. https://doi.org/10.1187/cbe.18-12-0238.

Examples on measuring scientific literacy

Examples reprinted with permission from publisher and author: Gormally, Cara, Peggy Brickman, and Mary Lutz. "Developing a Test of Scientific Literacy Skills (TOSLS): Measuring Undergraduates' Evaluation of Scientific Information and Arguments." Edited by Elisa Stone. CBE—Life Sciences Education 11, no. 4 (December 2012): 364–77. https://doi.org/10.1187/cbe.12-03-0026.

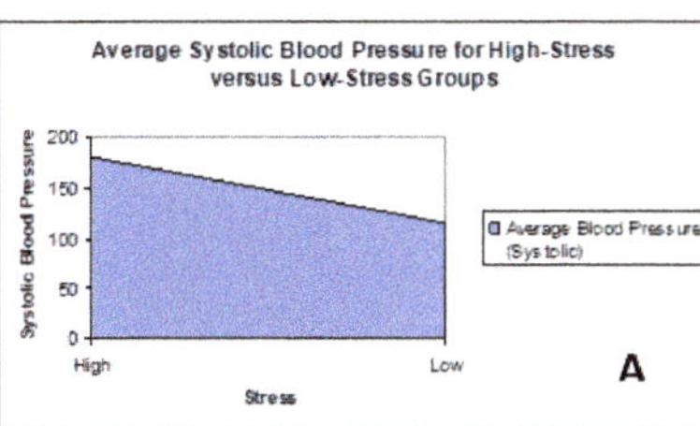

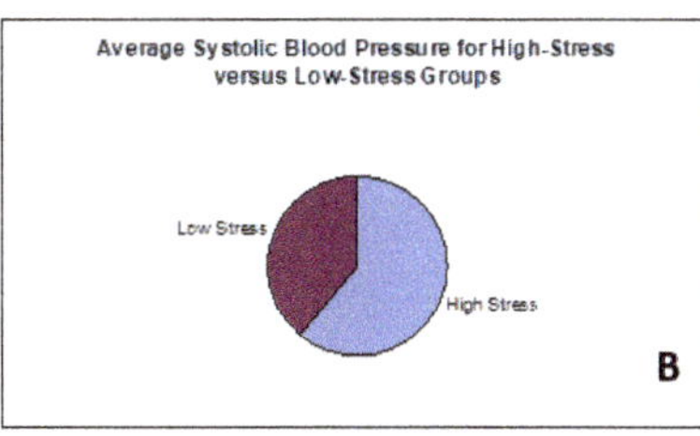

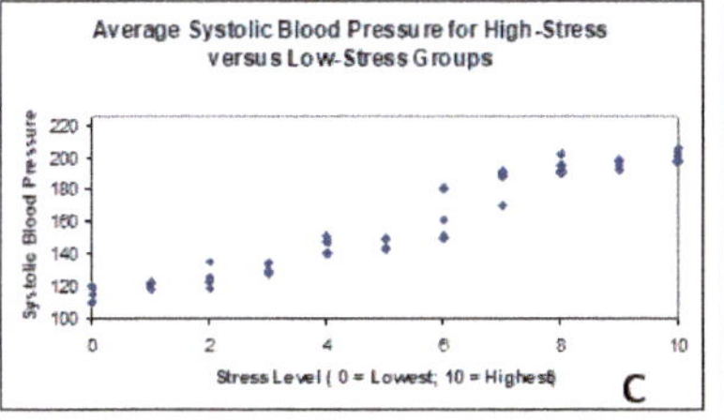

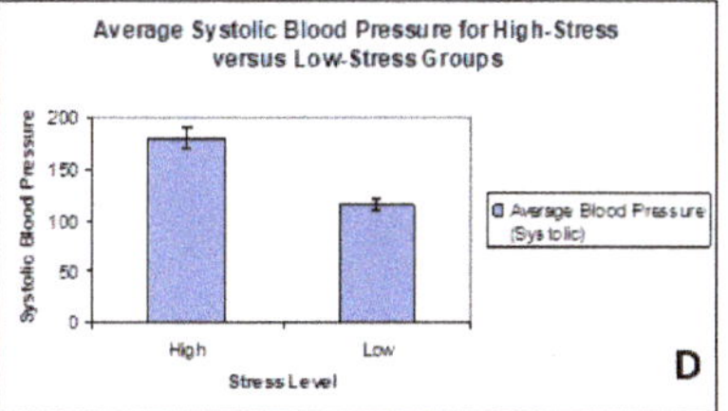

To detect the citizens' level of scientific literacy, it is useful to conduct a test at the beginning and end of a project, and thereby be able to evaluate the progression in scientific literacy. These tests are specifically useful when schools or educational institutions are involved. The citizen science projects can be part of or a supplement of their curriculum. Below are examples from the Test of Scientific Literacy Skills (TOSLS) used for undergraduate students. In this test, they must organise, analyse, and interpret quantitative data and scientific information.

1. Which of the following is a valid scientific argument?

   a. Measurements of sea level on the Gulf Coast taken this year are lower than normal; the average monthly measurements were almost 0.1 cm lower than normal in some areas. These facts prove that sea level rise is not a problem.

   b. A strain of mice was genetically engineered to lack a certain gene, and the mice were unable to reproduce. Introduction of the gene back into the mutant mice restored their ability to reproduce. These facts indicate that the gene is essential for mouse reproduction.

   c. A poll revealed that 34% of Americans believe that dinosaurs and early humans co-existed because fossil footprints of each species were found in the same location. This widespread belief is appropriate evidence to support the claim that humans did not evolve from ape ancestors.

   d. This winter, the northeastern US received record amounts of snowfall, and the average monthly temperatures were more than 2°F lower than normal in some areas. These facts indicate that climate change is occurring.

2. Researchers found that chronically stressed individuals have significantly higher blood pressure compared to individuals with little stress. Which graph would be most appropriate for displaying the mean (average) blood pressure scores for high-stress and low-stress groups of people?